GUDBYE NI RIZAL

And Other Poems and Hymns

Juan C. Nabong Jr.

Trafford rev. 06/04/2013

 www.trafford.com

North America & international
toll-free: 1 888 232 4444 (USA & Canada)
fax: 812 355 4082

CONTENTS

ANTECEDENTS TO GUDBYE NI RIZAL

The Internet holds abundant information on DR. JOSE P. RIZAL, the National Hero of the Republic of the Philippines. His autobiography, life, works, writings, learning, wisdom, and genius may be found in the pages of the Wikipedia, The Free Encyclopedia, Google, and Yahoo, JoseRizal, Ph website, and other websites.

On his second trip to Europe, he traveled from February 3, 1888, Manila to Hong Kong, to Amoy, to Yokohama in Japan, then on April 28, 1888 to San Francisco, then to Utah, Ogden, Denver, Salt Lake City, Colorado, Nebraska, Omaha, Chicago in Illinois, Albany, and ending his United States sojourn in New York on May 13, 1888. From there he then proceeded to Europe boarding the boat "City of Rome", reaching Queenstown, Ireland on May 24, 1888. In this brief interlude in the United States, he saw Niagara Falls, the Missouri River, Statue of Liberty, Golden Gate Bridge, and Reno.

Four of the greatest Renaissance Men who bequeathed everlasting honor and renown to their countries and to the world are Asians, born in the decade of the 1860s: RABINDRANATH TAGORE (May 7, 1861 – August 7, 1941), The First Asian to win the Nobel Prize for Literature in 1913; SUN YAT-SEN (November 12, 1866 – March 12, 1925), the Father of the Chinese Revolution, Founder of Modern China; MOHANDAS KARAMCHAND GANDHI (October 2, 1869 – January 30, 1948), whom Tagore called "The Great Soul" (Mahatma), who walked to Road to Freedom and Independence for India paved with Satya (Truth) and Ahimsa (Non-Violence, Peace, Love); and DR. JOSE P. RIZAL (born June 19, 1861), The National Hero of the Philippines, Eclectic Patriot and Man of Diverse Talents, Who Loved and Laid Down His Life and Dreams for His Family, Country, and Friends, Wielding Truly A Pen Mightier Than The Sword, and at Thirty Five Years Old Welcoming Death By Firing Squad (The Youngest of these Invincible and Enduring Asians) in the

Bagumbayan Field (Luneta now) on the early morn of December 30, 1896, Forever in the Hearts and Minds of Filipinos, Ever the Pride of Asians!

On the night of his death by firing squad, in Fort Santiago where he was imprisoned, Rizal wrote his last poem. When he was visited by his mother and sisters Josefa, Trinidad, and Lucia, he told his sisters in English that he had placed something in an alcohol lamp which he handed to them. In the afternoon after the Luneta execution, his sister Narcisa opened the alcohol lamp and lo! and behold! she found Rizal's poem!

The poem had no title but was later known "Mi Ultimo Adios". There are no less than 35 English translations, the most popular came from an American, Charles Derbyshire (1911). A translation by the Filipino National Artist Nick Joaquin (1944) can be found in the Rizal Park in Manila. This poem also bears 46 Filipino translations and has been translated in at least 37 other languages: Indonesian, Bengali, Bulgarian, Burmese, Chinese, Danish, Dutch, Fijian, French, German, Greek, Hawaiian, Hebrew, Hindi, Hungarian, Igbo (Nigeria), Italian, Japanese, Javanese, Korean, Latin, Maori, Norwegian, Portuguese, Romanian, Russian, Sanskrit, Sinhalese (Sri Lanka), Somali, Tahitian, Thai, Tongan, Turkish, Urdu (Pakistan), Vietnamese, Wolof (Senegal), and Yoruba (Nigeria) (Wikipedia, The Free Encyclopedia; Derbyshire's work was sold at The Philippine Education Company, Quiapo, Manila, circa 1965). (To Wikipedia, the farewell poem was given a title in Hong Kong (1897) by J.P.Braga, a publisher. There is a Wikipedia Philippines (English and Tagalog); there is a Google Philippines, Google Pilipinas, Google.com.ph sa English, and one offered in Filipino).

During his Asian Tour, President George W. Bush, like what other leaders from different nations do, visited the Rizal Monument in Manila to pay his respects to the Philippine National Hero Jose P. Rizal on Saturday, October 18, 2003, thereafter to address the Philippine Congress, and meet with President Gloria Macapagal-Arroyo (see photos of the wreath-laying at the Wikipedia by AFP/Jay Directo and AP Photo/Charles Dharapak).

GUDBYE NI RIZAL is crafted in a mix of the English, Pilipino and Tagalog, ample parts in text language, in modern idiom, with splashes of slang. Rizal speaks to YOU in your language today and in idiom you use because many have forgotten Rizal and so many do not even know him, and those who know him no longer cared for what he lived, stood, and died for.

Open your hearts and minds to reverberate once again to the touch and tremor of his thoughts, deeds, and writings, and harken to the words of our National Hero, for:

"He is Pepe, fine man," like you, my friend,
Will someday speak, as if you knew him by the heart
And even tell: "Yes, Jose Rizal, great Filipino,"
Though softly in your crowd.

....

"Must I now ask if death will finish him as mere a man
Or as one Filipino who truly loved his only land?
Do you not think, my friend, that, after all,
It is a charming, noble land?"

BAGONG BAYAN
(A New Nation)

Seven poems were published in the Philippines. Two are in the Internet, in poetry.com, and The International Library of Poetry (which recently published two books of poetry, Timeless Voices, Editor, Mr. Howard Ely, where the poem "Pushcart Baby: A Tale in Manila" appears and Forever Spoken, where "Love Text" is included)

In this collection, the author uses his pen names Johnny N., Jammer K., Ulilangkoboy, and Medardo Kalayaan.

My eleven-year old grandson Justin interpreted with a drawing Lindbergh's flight in his plane, The Spirit of St. Louis, from New York to Paris across the Atlantic (Justin has been to New York and when he was in Paris, saw the Eiffel Tower).

Brother-in-law of my wife, Mauro (Bibot) Ignacio, an Architect-Artist-Designer translates and interprets Rizal's martyrdom. He immersed himself in the study of the life of the Hero and centered his thoughts and vision on a rendering of the poem "Bagong Bayan".

To Adelina Hristova and Chrisel N. Cruz, for such patient, clean, and meticulous typing of the drafts and manuscripts of my books, specially so when I wrote the first drafts in longhand; for the final hardcopy and disk typing and editing which my daughter Pamela did with care and dispatch; and Miggy my grandson was always there handling the initial computer print for the disks, "Rossano "Autista" Nabong, my nephew and Beth, who took the picture of the Bust of Rizal at Lake Eola, Orlando, Florida.

A Big Thank You to All of You!!!

And ever and always my immense gratitude to my parents JUAN NABONG and ROSALINA S. CRUZ, my wife ZENAIDA (ZEN) CARRILLO, my sisters ESTER and her husband CESAR T. ABIERA, Sr., BELEN and her husband JOSE FESTIN (Pepe), EDNA LEE and husband REINO (Rei) LESADA and MARION and JUANITO (Johnny) BULACLAC, my brothers ORLANDO and DAVID, his wife BETHSAIDA (Betsy), DIMAGUIBA, and their respective sons and daughters, my children and grandchildren, sons and daughters-in-law, all kin and kith, JUAN

MONTGOMERY (Monty), PAMELA (Pamel, Pam), GILIW CARMEN (Diw), ANDREW JOSE (Budoy), CECILIA (Cecille), ADELINA, RUSSELL, MON, JOY, RYAN, and my grandsons and granddaughters TIMOTHY MARC, MARIA (Tricia), JUAN MIGUEL (Miggy), CRISEL, CJ, JUSTIN, JB, and the indefatigable hyper five-year old BEBKA.

Before I close I must also convey my inexhaustible thanks to my Fraternity Brothers in the Sigma Rho Fraternity, College of Law, University of the Philippines: to Sigma Rhoan Senator Edgardo J. Angara who commissioned Brod Joe Abejo and I to come up with The IBP Hymn; to Grand Archons of the Fraternity, Jose Aruego and Wenceslao "Pee Wee" Trinidad who appointed us to create The Sigma Rho Hymn; and to Congressman Aniceto "Dong" Saludo, Jr. (Southern Leyte) who requested me to write the lyrics of The University of the Philippines Law Alumni Association Diamond Jubilee Hymn, with Dean Prof. Ramon Santos of the U.P. College of Music fashioning the music, the choral rendition provided by the Conservatory's Charivari Choir.

Thanks also to my colleagues and friends at the Philippine Christian University, Adamson University, Ortanez University, and the Polytechnic University of the Philippines, where I taught through the years. It was at Adamson when we founded and established The Philippine Jury Movement. My gratitude also goes to my friends and co-movers at the YMCA, Y's Men Club of Manila, Philippine Lawyers Association, Parapsychological Club of the Philippines, Philippine Constitution Association, ALA, LAWASIA, Philippine Historical Association, National Register of Prominent Americans and International Notables, Translators Committee of the Philippines, now TAP, Filipino Counterpart of the Summer Institute of Linguistics, IBP, Manila IV, World Fraternity of Lawyers, Knox Memorial Methodist Church Official Board, Rotary Club of Iligan and Rotary Club of Uptown Manila, my fellow delegates at the Asian Mass Communications Research and Information Center Conference, Chiang Mai, Thailand, 1981, and in 1995, International Discourse on Dr. Jose P. Rizal held at Malaysia, Kuala Lumpur. Thanks too for the fun, friendship, and dedicated rehearsals with my Brethren and Sisters at the Scottish Rite Chorale (Brothers of Harmony & Ladies of Melody), Luzon Bodies Choir, Hiram Lodge Choir, UHSM Choir, Solicitor General's Office Choir, and the Knox Memorial Methodist Church Choir. Modesty aside, I was a basketball player, center, UHSM Team, and a weekly finalist of the Radio

Show "Melody Club" hosted by Leila Benitez and Pinggoy Pecson, then the Filipino version of the American Idol.

My beloved classmates (U.P. Law '58) I'll always, ever remember you who are here and those who have gone "to that Undiscovered Country where no Traveller returns" but are no strangers to Angels inhabiting that Glorious, Awesome World of Worlds with no more Toils, Tears, Fears!

What a great blessing to my life that I joined the Order of the Knights of Rizal, "A Civic, Patriotic and Cultural Non-Sectarian Non-Partisan Organization Chartered Under Republic Act No. 646" some thirty-three years ago. My late father had been a member since 1961. My first book GIRD LIFE WITH THE TRUTH, A Filipino Father Life's Episodes, narrates his Initiation into the Order.

"Father was initiated a Knight of Rizal at the Goldenberg Mansion on December 28, 1961 with SK Samuel Capistrano, Sir Knight Aurelio Mendoza, SK Gerardo Armonio, SK Alfredo Cathedral, SK Jose Yap, and SK Mariano Alimurong. This is the international fraternal Order of those who propagate the life, works, ideals, and virtues of our National Hero, Dr. Jose P. Rizal." (Page 64; refer also to No. 33, page 127, No. 40, p. 133, and pages 40-41) He had a bust of Rizal on his office table.

I was introduced to our National Hero when I was Grade Six participating in a Rizal Oratorical Contest in the Lakan-Dula Elementary School in Tondo, Manila. My teacher-coach explained the poem "The Song of the Traveller" while teaching me the rudiments of good oration. I won first prize! What an incredible, jubilant moment to a twelve-year old!

In 1992 Sir Johnny F. Goloyugo, KCR, invited me to be a member of the Order's International Chapter, Manila.

Since my membership in the two Chapters, I've had the opportunity to meet the great leadership of the Order and Chapters join their exciting, satisfying, and ennobling activities, events, assemblies, and celebrations.

I deeply nurture the memories and glorious times I've had at the Lakan-Dula Elementary School in Tondo, Manila (pre-WWII and early Liberation), Arellano and Union High Schools of Manila, U.P. College of Law, Diliman, Quezon City, Manuel L. Quezon University School of Graduate Studies (Ll.M.), University of Santo Tomas Graduate School

(D.C.L.), Centro Escolar University (all in Manila), City of Manila where I, as City Administrator, worked with Mayor Mel Lopez, and Jim Lopez who became a three-term, well-liked Congressman of Manila (Tondo II), fellow Attorneys and Section Chiefs at the Claro M. Recto Law Offices at Intramuros, Manila, fellow Judges and personnel in the Regional Trial Court of Lanao del Norte, Branch I, Iligan City, Mindanao and Regional Trial Court of Manila, Branch 32. I never forget, but sincerely appreciate, the unwavering help, support, trust, and guidance given me by the Honorable Solicitor General, Minister, and Governor Estelito and Rose Mendoza, Supreme Court Justice and Global Arbitrator, Honorable Vicente and Mrs. Thelma Mendoza, The Honorable Chief Justice Reynato and Luz Puno, Supreme Court of the Philippines, the Methodist Church Parliamentarian and Judge Isaac S. Puno, Jr. and his wife Rosella Jean.

The enchantment and dearest moments I shared with you during my young years, school years, young adult life, professional life, and now in my golden years, reverberate in my heart and mind. Unending Thanks, You and Family, Ever!!!

In early October, 2007 a close family friend, Frank Banzon, called to invite me to attend a Knight of Rizal meeting of theirs. Knight of Rizal! And I have not attended one for such a long, long time, after I retired from Judicial Service! I gladly agreed, that was my introduction to you Sirs and Ladies. I felt accepted, glad, thanks Sir Frank and to you my Brother Knights and Sister Ladies, thanks for extending your hand of friendship, camaraderie, and generous hospitality in your ORDER OF THE KNIGHTS OF RIZAL, CENTRAL FLORIDA CHAPTER.

I may have missed many, many names whom I have not thanked and acknowledged. My deepest apologies.............

The journey has been roughed and rugged at times, many times, but YOU, WITH GOD'S GRACE AND COMPASSION, were always there to lighten the paths and heal the burdens...............

JUAN C. NABONG JR.

April 10, 2010

Orlando, Florida

AK AND NETTIE

For Sarah Aleck Bovick,
Friend

AK and Nettie hold and amuse their children
In their garden. Nettie, the Neferet, Queen of Kemet, hemet of AK,
Blooms as the lotus blossoms in her paradise, her sechemech-ib.
But uneasy questionings creep in their Kingdom
As AK decrees, for the first time:
"There shall be no netsheru here, no worship of many gods!
Only Aten shall be the god; and when you see Aten
In the sky, you see our god, the good god for the people!"
Nettie died ahead of her Pharaoh, and when he died
The wabs and their syndicates, clipped of their powers under AK,
Accused AK of having ruled against Maat, a disease to the land
Of many gods. AK died remembering Nettie's words
In their garden, "As the rays of Aten's sun-disc in the sky shines on us,
You and I, our family, our children, will be together, forever!"

I look at your bust, Nettie, found in an unknown sculptor's workplace
(Circa 1340 BC). What eternally stunning, supremely beautiful face!
I gaze at you Nettie and I, too, belly drum as if I'm eating dates and figs,
Berries, pomegranates, olives, cheese, quails, pigeons, grilled ox ribs,
And drinking barley beer. Oh! I smell myrrh and incense, ivy, lotus
blossoms
As a depet carries me gliding on the Nile......ahhh......this...is...Ankh!!!

Johnny N.

Manila, Philippines, 2004

ABAY LOVES INAY LOVES ABAY

(Dad Loves Mom Loves Dad)

I placed
Flowers
At Mothers' grave
In Chicago's Rosehill Cemetery
And, prayed.

Before leaving,
I picked
A few
For Fathers' tomb
In the La Loma
Cementerio del Norte,
In Manila,
Philippines.

Ulilangkoboy

Composed
At the Rosehill Cemetery
In Chicago, September 8, 1997

Father and Mother

GUDBYE NI RIZAL

GUDBYE AKING BAYAN, ATING BAYAN,
4GOTTEN STRANGER, BLESSED NI GOD
SA SILANGAN, IBANG IBA CYA! SAYO'Y IHA2TAG
ANG SOBRANG INAPI KONG BUHAY,
MBWI AT MATAMO MO LNG ANG NINA2SANG KALAYAAN.

SA WAR MAT PATAYAN, NAPAKARAMING NAGBUWIS NG
BUHAY.
KHIT NA SAANG D MALAMANG LIBINGAN TUMUMBA:
SA GARROTE, BITAY, GITNA NG BULAKLAK,
O, PARANG, NANGAMATAY CLA,
AT ANG TINAMO AY LURAY-LURAY NA PANAGINIP
SA BUHAY NA INIALAY SA PAMILYA 'T BAYANG MINAHAL.

MLAPIT NA, DEDO NKO, MOMENT OF TRUTH NA2.
OOOOOHHH! SUMISILIP NA ANG ARAW!
GUS2 MO B ANG PULANG KOLOR PRA SUMIKLAB
ANG KAGANDAHAN MO? HETO, DUGO KO
IBUDBOD MO. AYAN, PINAKA-MLIWANAG
ANG TILANSIK NG BRYTNEZ MO!
MALA-VAN GOGH ANG DATING!

MUSMOS HANGGANG TINAYGER,
PANAGINIP KO'Y ISANG MLAYANG PILIPINAS,
WLANG HINAGPIS, WALANG KAHI2YAN, WALANG DUDA,
D TAKOT, NO SURRENDER I2 PARDS! NO CHOICE.
MATIRA ANG MATIBAY NA PANAGINIP, DO OR DIE!

MABUHAY KA! MABUHAY KA! ANG MSSG KO:
KHIT MMTAY MAN AKO MABUHAY KA LAMANG PILIPINAS,
MAHI2MBING NRIN AKONG 2NAY SA KALUPAAN MO,
WINNING MOMENT KO NA2!

F 1 BULAKLAK
SA PUNTOD KO'Y GUMAWI,
JAZ HUG N HAGKAN MO2, IMAGINE MO AKO'Y SYA,
MLSAP KO NMAN YARING KISMO, DAT U KERR,
DAT U SHARE LAB, HART 2 HART TAYO 2GEDER,
NPKSWIT MONG TLGA IYONG IYO AKO SYO 4EVER!

HAYAAN MONG I KAIBIGAN LUMUHA
SA MAAGA KONG KMTYAN,
AT PAMINSAN-MINSAN, SA KTAHIMIKAN,
KUNG AKO'Y PINAPANALANGIN,
PANALANGIN MO RIN ANG ANAK MO, INANG BAYAN,
NA SA PILING NI ALMIGHTY BATHALA
MMMAHINGA NRIN AT......MALILIMUTAN.

IPAGDASAL YUNG MGA NASAWI,
NALUSAW SA PIGHATI, MGA INA,
MAHAPDI'T MAPAKLA ANG LUHA;
IPAGDASAL ANG BALO, ULILA, OPPRESSED,
BILANGGONG TORTURED: MAGDASAL, AT MATINDING
ITIMPLA:
KALIGTASAN, KARAPATAN, ASAP!

AT KUNG DUMILIM NA SA LIBINGAN,
AT ANG NANGAMATAY NLANG ANG NAGMA2SID,
ANG DI MO GETS WAG ARUKIN;
AT KUNG DITO'Y MAY NARINIG NA UMAAWIT,
AKO YUN, BAYANG LABS KO, ENCHANTING U WITH A
LENNON LULLABY.

F ANG GRAVE KO AY 4GOTTEN NA BY OL,
TSAKA WLA MAN LNG KRUZ O LPIDA UPANG AKO'Y
MAALALA,
ARARUHIN I2, BUTO AT ABO KO'Y IKALAT,
UPANG KALAWAKAN NMAY MHAGKANG KONG 2NAY!

D BALE RING 4GETS MOKO, BAYAN AT KAIBIGAN, OK LNG.
MLAYA KO NMANG MAKA2LAGUYO ANG LAWAK NG
LANGIT MO,
BUNDOK MO, DAGAT, BTIS, PAMPANG, ILOG,
PAMANTASAN, ESKWELA SA BARRIO, KWEBA,
KUTA, FACTORIES, RICEFIELDS, SUPERHIGHWAYS,
EDSA, LRT, ISKWATERS AT DUMPSITES,
URBAN AREAS, NVIRONMENT CENTERS,
MALLS, KARISMATIK FLOCKS, SUBDIVISIONS,
AND CONDOS; MAGIGING HIMIG, BANGO,
TAMIS, LATIK, AT HALIK NG PAG-ASA'T PANA2MPALATAYA'Y
UULIT-ULITIN, HANEP!

MINIMITHI KONG BANSA, ELO!
OOOOOHHH! PINAS! GUDBYE,
2U I LEAVE EVERYTHING:
MAGULANG, MGA MINAMAHAL.
GO AKO SA WLANG SLAVES, WALANG ABUSADO,
ARGABYADO, WALANG DICTADOR, TRAIDOR,
SUWABENG TERRORISTA, DUN ALIVE ANG FAITH,
VALUES, INTEGRITY, LIBERTY, AND JUSTICE!
C GOD LANG ANG SUPERHARI!!!

GUDBYE MAGULANG KO, BRODS,
KABA2TA SA SINUGATANG THANAN.
MAGPASLAMAT KYO COZ MA2MAHINGA NKO.
PAGUUUUUD NA PAGUD NA ME!
GUDBYE MY BLUE-EYED WITH CHESTNUT HAIR
EXTRANJERA---JOSEPHINE, FREN KO, KA M.U. KO,
MHAL NA MHAL KTA AWESOME BEAUTY YOU!
MIZNAMIZKTA MY RESTLESS GOLONDRINA!
ILAW, KULAY, SIGAW, TIGIDIG KA NG PUSO KO!!
GUDBYE, LABS KO OL KYO!
HALIKANA KAMATAYAN, HALIKANA…YAKAPIN MO NA
KO…
NOW MAKA2PAGPA2HINGA NA RIN AT LAST!
HIRAM LNG NMAN NTIN KE GOD I2NG BUHAY NA2.
TOL, KAIBIGAN, YNGATZ K PLAGI, I'VE GOT TO GO,
K1TYO, GODBLESS……….GUDNAYT……….g'nayt…………

JAMMER K

DECEMBER 30, 2002

7

RIZAL'S GOOD-BYE

(A FREE AND UNHAMPERED RENDERING
OF GUDBYE NI RIZAL)

GOODBYE MY COUNTRY, OUR COUNTRY,
FORGOTTEN STRANGER, BLESSED BY GOD.
IN THE EAST, HOW AMAZINGLY DIFFERENT! TO YOU
I BEQUETHED MY RELENTLESSLY OPPRESSED LIFE
THAT YOU MAY REACH OUR DESIRED FREEDOM.

IN WAR OR KILLINGS,
SO MANY HAVE GIVEN THEIR LIVES;
IN UNKNOWN GRAVES THEY HAVE FALLEN:
BY GARROTE, BY HANGING, IN THE MIDST OF FLOWERS
OR HILLS THEY HAD DIED,
SACRIFICING LIVES, REAPING TATTERED DREAMS,
FOR FAMILY AND BELOVED LAND.

IT'S NEAR AND SOON I WILL BE DEAD. THIS IS THE
MOMENT OF TRUTH,
OOOOOHHH! THE SUN SMILINGLY PEEPS IN THE HORIZON!
WOULD YOU LIKE A RED COLOR TO ENHANCE YOUR
BEAUTY?
HERE, SCATTER MY BLOOD!
HOW CLEAR YOUR BRIGHTNESS WILL SPREAD!
OOHH MY! IT OOZES LIKE A VAN GOGH!

FROM EARLY TOT TO TEENAGER I'VE ALWAYS DREAMT
OF A FREE PHILIPPINES WITHOUT SORROWS, WITH NO
SHAME,
WITHOUT DOUBT; NEVER FEARFUL; WITHOUT
SURRENDERING,
NO CHOICE, MAY THIS DREAM SURVIVE, DO OR DIE!

LONG LIVE! LONG LIVE! HERE'S MY MESSAGE:
E'EN THOUGH I DIE AS LONG AS YOU SHALL LIVE MY
PHILIPPINES,
I WILL TRULY BE AT REST IN MY NATIVE LAND.
THIS IS MY WINNING MOMENT!

IF ONE FLOWER VISITS ME ON MY GRAVE,
JUST HUG AND KISS IT, IMAGINE I AM THIS FLOWER,
LET ME SAVOR YOUR KISS AND KNOW THAT YOU CARE,
THAT YOU SHARE LOVE WITH ME, HEART TO HEART,
TOGETHER,
YOU'RE SO REAL SUPER SWEET, I'M YOURS FOREVER!

LET A FRIEND SHED TEARS AT MY EARLY DEATH,
AND ONCE IN A WHILE, IN THE SILENCE,
IF I'M OFFERED A PRAYER,
PLEASE PRAY ALSO FOR YOUR SON, MY MOTHERLAND,
THAT IN THE BOSOM OF MY ALMIGHTY GOD
I WILL BE AT REST AT LAST AND…BE FORGOTTEN.

PRAY FOR THOSE WHO DIED,
WHO GRIEVE; THOSE MOTHERS,
BITTER AND HURTING, ARE THEIR TEARS;
PRAY FOR THE WIDOWS, ORPHANS, THE OPPRESSED,
IMPRISONED, TORTURED: PRAY AND MIGHTILY PLAN:
FREEDOM, RIGHTS, NOW!

AND WHEN DARKNESS DESCENDS UPON MY GRAVE
AND ONLY THE DEAD WATCH;
DELVE NOT INTO WHAT YOU DON'T UNDERSTAND.

BUT WHEN YOU HEAR SOMEONE SINGING,
I AM THAT SINGER, MY BELOVED LAND,
ENCHANTING YOU WITH A LENNON LULLABY.

WHEN MY GRAVE IS THEN FORGOTTEN BY ALL,
AND THERE IS NO MORE CROSS OR MEMORIAL TABLET
TO REMEMBER ME BY, PLOW MY REMAINS,
SCATTER MY BONES AND ASHES TO THE WINDS
SO I CAN KISS THIS ENORMOUS, ETERNAL UNIVERSE!

IF YOU FORGET ME, BELOVED LAND AND FRIENDS, IT'S
ALL RIGHT,
BUT I WILL BE FREE TO CARESS THE HEAVENS,
YOUR MOUNTAINS, SEAS, CREEKS, BEACHES, RIVERS,
UNIVERSITIES, SCHOOLS IN HINTERLANDS, EVEN CAVES
FORTS, FACTORIES, FARMS, SUPERHIGHWAYS,
THE EDSA, LRTS, SQUATTERS, DUMPSITES, URBAN AREAS,
ENVIRONMENTAL CENTERS, MALLS,
CHARISMATIC FLOCKS, SUBDIVISIONS
AND CONDOS; YIELDING MUSIC, BEWITCHING SCENT,
SWEETNESS, AND HONEY-GLAZED KISSES OF HOPES
AND FAITH AGAIN AND AGAIN. UNBELIEVABLE!

MY ADORED AND CHERISHED NATION, HELLO!
OOOOOHHH! PHILIPPINES! GOOD-BYE!
TO YOU I LEAVE EVERYTHING: MY PARENTS AND LOVED
ONES
I GO WHERE SLAVES THERE ARE NONE, NO ABUSERS
PROSPER,
NONE ARE OPPRESSED, NO DICTATORS, TRAITORS,
OR COOL TERRORISTS. THERE, FAITH, VALUES,
INTEGRITY, LIBERTY, AND JUSTICE THRIVE,
WITH GOD ONLY AS THE SUPREME KING!!!

GOOD-BYE MY PARENTS, BRODS,
CHILDHOOD CHUMS IN THE SHATTERED HOUSE
AND WOUNDED HOME. BE THANKFUL BECAUSE I WILL
NOW REST.
I AM SO TIRED, SO……TIRED……
GOOD-BYE MY BLUE-EYED WITH CHESTNUT HAIR
FOREIGNER--------SWEET JOSEPHINE, MY CHERISHED
COMPANION,
I LOVE YOU SO MUCH AWESOME BEAUTY YOU!
YOU'RE MY ONE AND ONLY I MISS YOU SO MUCH
MY RESTLESS GOLONDRINA! YOU'RE THE LIGHT, THE
COLOR,
THE THRILLS AND TINGLE, THE RHYME AND RHYTHM
OF MY HEART!
GOOD-BYE I LOVE YOU ALL SO MUCH!
COME NOW DEATH, COME NOW……EMBRACE ME
NOW…….
NOW, AT LAST, I….CAN….REST!
OUR LIFE IS ONLY BORROWED FROM GOD.

BROTHER, FRIEND, TAKE CARE ALWAYS, I'VE GOT TO GO.
WE ARE ONE, GODBLESS……..GOOD NIGHT……g'night…….

                                             JAMMER K.

JUNE 30, 2006
ORLANDO, FLORIDA

BAGONG BAYAN

Let him stand and let him bear the fire of guns
That hover now in these grounds where a crowd watches
A man about to be shot this December morning
Past another dawn. Note his face for you may love
His calm of heart; learn of his thoughts
So you may know the grief behind his pen and deeds,
The sorrows of a land, his land,
The tragic people of his works and poems,
The throbs of freedom in his heart.

This man---Rizal---he has to die so he can never smite
Our Spain again. He was tried and judged: he has incited fellow Indios
Here and there to revolt against our authority of force,
Our plans, our laws. His fight, though not in categories
Of guns and blood, was nonetheless so caustic,
So subversive, so hard against our Church, her friars
And our rule. His pen gave us much worries;
Very irritating to our clan. He wrote and what he wrote
Did surely gird his countrymen to desire and die
For tempting liberty, for privilege for his class, you know.
Some die-hard, bigoted nationalist, this guy.
You'll even wonder that the love and the dedication
He invested upon his land were more than all the romancing
He had smoothed upon his women of many foreign tongues!

And much more, friend, he has a knack to goad the young ones
And even women of a local place to forge on with their struggles
Against the dictates of our policies, fancying that one day
Soon, their country will be theirs alone. He must accept
That this will never, never be, for now or then.

We will have to shatter all these dreams and dawns to dirt.
These indios are now turning to a fighting race;
They are getting pretty plenty from his seditious pen
And words, to say the least!

12

For sure another year is here, my friend.
I tell you now they're getting angrier each day
To push through thick-and-thin their fight.
More fights are coming up again, I have to say.
I do not know if there shall be within this coming year
Or so, more local blood to litter towns and streets
And fields. Of course, we have to hammer down
Their brown-burned guts our rule and might
Or else more men like him will daunt and dare
The dominions of our Cross and Country.

This day, however, is bound to be a history
Of Spanish jubilation. We shoot this stubborn man,
To ground he falls, just like the rest of rebels
To cut their petty urge for freedom,
Their vice for liberty. But, you know, what amazing discontent I find
In these masses! And yet, if I may say:
This man is lucky man indeed; we do not shoot him
Like the others then and there. At least, he has a crowd
Who'll watch, including chums, I guess.

Kill him then, my civil friends.
But will that end the movement of his thoughts
And spirit that have already found their strong soil
In his Noli, Fili books, his Liga aims, the various poems
And essays, letters, and writings in his years
Away from home? Will that fizzle out the illusions
Of redemption of these bitter, disgusted peoples
As they howl in revolt for rights, peace and freedom
Into their farms and homes? Come now my friend, do you mean
To make me understand that, with his focused nationalist path
We can still rest easy and just leave it
To our guns and our Cross of force to stop
Their thrilling faith and fight? Now, now, you think this man
Will fear he's rather dying young? Will he not think, you ask,

That after all his work for emancipation, for dignity, and equality,
He'll fall to darkness and die alone? A pity, you muse,
At such a cultured man to die so young. Then, accustom him
In your turn of history to merely think of early summers
With his Calamba folks of home; of friends in foreign lands;
The women of his seas and songs; his friends over here;
Forget the rage of Katipuneros and faraway fellowmen
Who also espouse the same sad visions of a free
And rightful land to inhabit above the necessities of our bullets,
Firing squads, our unversatile colonial policies
And our decadent parochial minds. You still insist that,
In his common death and fall, a final tremor shall spear
The hearts of his countrymen to cower and despair
Before our terrific might?

There; they're going to shoot him now at last.
I heard of someone in the crowd just now who said:
"He is Pepe; fine man," like you, my friend,
Will someday speak, as if you knew him by the heart
And even tell: "Yes, Jose Rizal; great Filipino,"
Though softly in your crowd. It is as if he will not be alone
To die and bear his handsome death for long.
Another year and years are coming up.
A whole, new, nation was his vision through his years,
And by that flame, he had to die. And live in your heart and mine.

Must I now ask if death will finish him as mere a man
Or as one Filipino who truly loved his only land?
Do you not think, my friend, that, after all,
It is a charming, noble land?

Medardo Kalayaan

Manila, Philippines
January 1964

REMEMBER LINDBERGH DID IT!

Losing roots of courage? Grasping only the wasted left-over dreams?
Where is life leading you Miss Depressed, Mr. Despairing?
But remember young man and young woman, Lindbergh did it!
At twenty-seven, by his guts, perseverance, and constancy
America's Youth made a thrilling difference in the world!

On May 21, 1927, twenty-seven year old Lindbergh
Flew his plane - The Spirit of St. Louis -
(Wingspan - 14 meters (46 ft.); Length - 8 meters (27'8");
And Engine - Wright Whirlwind J 5C, 223 hp)
From Roosevelt Field, Long Island, New York,
To Bourget Field in Paris, France,
In 33 hours, 30 minutes, and in this plane
Manufactured by the Ryan Airlines Co.
(N. Y. 211, Ryan N.Y.P), (Wow! At D.C. in '82 I saw that modest plane
Hanging in a corner ceiling inside the Smithsonian Institution!)
Lindbergh became the first man to cross the Atlantic
Of land, sea, and wind, in the First Solo Non-Stop Flight
Over 5810 kilometers (3610 miles)! Cool!

There is no cause to soak in hopelessness and despair.
Challenge the future!
Soar with faith and hope in life's highways and by-ways!
Their wonders are very yours! Conquer! Win!
Whether at twenty-seven or seventy-seven,
Move Earth and Heaven!
Remember Lindbergh did it!

JAMMER K.

Dallas, TX Summer '82

Picture of Charles A. Lindbergh taken in the Garden of The Cabilis (Brod Mayor Camilo Cabili and Sister Leni A. Cabili) during his visit to Mindanao (Iligan City) in 1972.

LAB TXT

WNT 2 D MUVIS BOT DVDS
HAD FUN @ DISNEY DROV D BC ROWDS
OF ORLANDO TUK KOPI @ BARNIES
BAT O BAT SADENLY M MISING U
DARLING NGEL SWIT NGEL
HU SAVD ME FRM DESPAYRING
3LLD MY WUNDED SHORS
WID UR GIPS OF SONGS
SOPEND WUNDS OF SORO N MY SOUL

MINITS W/U R NVR SO GLORYUS
DAYS NVR SO NCHANTING AS VAN GOGHS
SANFLAWERS U HIL BARDENS W/ KERR N SWITNES

MY INBOX S NATING W/OUT UR TXTS
OKYING D MIRAKELS OF UR VOIS
OPNING PATS 2 DRIMS & BRIGES
BITER JORNIS FRM MY OUTBOX
NOW GLADND 4EVRMOR

JOHNNY N.

April 28, 2001

LOVE TEXT

I WENT TO THE MOVIES; BOUGHT DVDs,
HAD FUN AT DISNEY; DROVE THE BUSY ROADS
OF ORLANDO, TOOK COFFEE AT BARNIES.
BUT, OH, BUT SUDDENLY I'M MISSING YOU
DARLING ANGEL! SWEET ANGEL!
WHO SAVED ME FROM DESPAIRING,
THRILLED MY WOUNDED SHORES
WITH YOUR GIFTS OF SONGS.
SOFTENED WOUNDS OF SORROW IN MY SOUL.

MINUTES WITH YOU ARE NEVER SO GLORIOUS.
NEVER SO ENCHANTING AS VAN GOGH'S
SUNFLOWERS. YOU HEAL BURDENS WITH CARE AND
SWEETNESS.

MY INBOX IS NOTHING WITHOUT YOUR TEXTS,
OKAYING THE MIRACLES OF YOUR VOICE,
OPENING PATHS TO DREAMS AND BRIDGES,
BITTER JOURNEYS FROM MY OUTBOX
NOW GLADDENED FOREVERMORE.

JOHNNY N.

April 28, 2001

ODE

(FOR PAT JAMES IN MANILA)

A SHIP BRINGING PEACE CORPS VOLUNTEERS
(TO INDIA AND ASIAN COUNTRIES)
DOCKED IN TRANSIT AT THE MANILA, PHILIPPINE PORT
YEARS AGO. IN THIS SHIP DURING A WELCOME PARTY,
I, YOUNG DREAMER, UNBEHOLDEN TO THE FUTURE,
MET YOU. IT MATTERED TOO LITTLE TO ME THEN
THAT YOUR HEART DWELT IN SERVING OTHER PEOPLES.
TO YOU, THE NAME OF TOMORROW
WERE THOSE DEPRIVED THIRD WORLD
STREETCHILDREN,
THE MALNOURISHED, THE POOR, SICK, AND HOMELESS
YOU HUNGERED TO HELP AND TO SAVE
THOUGH THEY BE FAR AWAY FROM YOUR DEAR HOME
IN CALIFORNIA. YOU HAD THE CONSTANCY, THE DESIRE,
TO SERVE, REKINDLING EMBERS OF FADING HOPES
AND FAILED DREAMS AND VISIONS.
OF LIFE'S BETTERMENT AND PROGRESS,
TO THEM, YOU WERE A MOTHER TERESA
ESTABLISHING A MISSION OF CHARITY AND COMPASSION
AT DEL PAN IN MANILA, A JOSEPHINE BRACKEN
EDUCATING THE YOUTH IN RIZAL'S BOYS SCHOOL
AT DAPITAN IN MINDANAO, OR A LADY DI CARING FOR
THE SICK
OR WOUNDED AT SAO PAOLO. BUT.....
WHAT MATTERED TO ME, THEN, WAS.......ONLY YOU!

OH, HOW I LONG AND CHERISH THAT.....OH THAT
ONE EVENING, ON THE DECK, BEFORE THE NERVOUS SEA
AND SINGING WIND WHEN YOU TENDERED YOUR
FRIENDSHIP
AND TOLD ME YOU TOO CARED FOR ME......AND.....
AND.....
ALL THE WEARINESS AND RESTLESSNESS
OF MY YOUTH WERE GONE!!!

I HOPE---MAY THIS FALTERING LITTLE NOTE
FIND YOU IN THIS VAST AMERICA---
TO BRING YOU ONCE MORE.....EVER.........
TO A FRIEND FROM MANILA.

                                        JOHNNY N.

CHICAGO
SEPTEMBER 8, 1997

HOLD FOREVER HER DEAR GOOD-BYE

FIND THE DREAM
    FIND ME THE LAUGHTER;
SEEK THE WARMTH
    OF A GIRL…HOW I'VE LOST HER SMILE!

BRING TENDERNESS
BRING ME THE GLADNESS
    OF ONE WHO SPOKE
    OF EARTH, PEACE,
      AND PLACES,
WHO SPOKE OF HEART,
    AND HOME.

SHE---YOUNG WIND,
    MY BLISS,
GARDEN OF MY THRILLS
    AND THROBS---
OH MY HEART AND HEAVES,
    HER KISS! I MISS!!!

FIND ME LONGING FOR A TOUCH, HER GAZE;
CLASP THE TEARS OF DAWN, OF THE MORNINGS'
    EMPTY ROOMS, WIDE HALLS;
I SIT ON THE EDGE OF MY BED, ALONE,
    AMAZED, GONE, HOLDING FOREVER
    HER DEAR GOOD-BYE.

                                      JOHNNY N.

ORLANDO, FL
OCTOBER 15, 1997

The authographs of the Dame Margot Fonteyn and Rudolf Nureyev were given to the author at their practice session at the Cultural Center of the Philippines on August 26, 1977. Dame Margot Fonteyn's authograph is on the left part of the envelop while Rudolf Nureyev's is on the middle to the right side portion.

JOSEPHINE B.

Josephine B.
Josephine Bracken

Josephine B., ampon ni Taufer,
Akay ang Taufer, dumating ang dalawa sa Dapitan
Pagagamot ang bulag na yatang mga mata ni Tatay
Sa exiled na Dr. Jose P. Rizal.

Isang tingin sa mata ni Tatay,
Isang tiingin din ni Doctor
Sa batang dalagang, blue-eyed,
Chestnut-haired extranjera!

Love at first sight na baga ito Doc?
Siya na ba, siya na ba? Kay Euro-Asian beauty na ba
Patungo ang everlasting love mo Doc?
But Josephine B. kailangan ka ni Tatay,
    No cure na sa mata nya.
Ibalik 'syang kasama ka sa Hong Kong
    At sa pinanggalingan. But…
Sa Manila lang si Taufer sinamahan.
Bumalik si Miss B. kay Rizal sa Dapitan,
Kasi na in-love na rin ang dalaga!

Leonor Rivera, Gunding Katigbak,
Orang Valenzuela, Filipina.
Connie Ortiga pa ring Española,
    May O-Sei-Kiyo-San pang Japonesa;
Tottie Beckett, Nellie Boustead,
Suzanne Jacoby all sa Europa.
Bakit ako pa? ask mo ampong lonely
Sad and forlorn na baga si Joe dito? Traveller yata 'yan!

Josephine B.
Josephine Bracken at si Rizal sa Talisay!

Kissing her beside that big rock
　　Near the seashore of Dapitan……..
Let's now marry here before the skies,
Before the sea, before the winds, before this earth,
And before God, my Restless Golondrina,
For authorities tell me: no, no, no, Doctor Rizal, no,
Mag-retract ka muna. I-retract mo ang mga isinulat
At ikinalat mo laban sa amin bago ka payagan ng simbahan
Magpakasal kay Miss Bracken. But…
Never, never, never will I demean
My freedom, my honor, my works, my rage!
I'm so alone here, oh how my country suffers
But tomorrow…someday…soon…
Our nation will be free!

Josephine B.
Josephine Bracken and Rizal all the way
　　Tulungan sa Talisay!

Sa bahay, sa boys school mo Joe,
　　Sa clinic at ospital,
Sa farm, sa business, tulungan tayong total;
Our future is here, home sweet home natin 'to.
"Never to part, heart bound to heart" tayo!
Nang namatay ang supling nating si Francisco,
God, bakit ang aming Little Rizal pa?

Malapit na, Fort Santiago na,
    Sa firing squad malapit na,
"Dear and unhappy wife" a year lamang
    Nakapiling ka; "Adios, Dulce Extranjera,
    Mi Amiga, Mi Alegria",
Farewell, paalam, goodbye Miss B.
"Your ever faithful and true till death."

Farewell Josephine B., mis na mis ka na,
Goodbye Josephine B., mahal na mahal kita!
I've got to go 'bye Jo.

                                                    Jammer K.

Manila, Philippines
November 10, 1991

JOSEPHINE B.

(A FREE AND SIMPLE RENDERING OF THE POEM
JOSEPHINE B. IN ENGLISH)

JOSEPHINE B.
JOSEPHINE BRACKEN.

JOSEPHINE B. ACCOMPANIED HER ADOPTIVE FATHER
TAUFER
TO DAPITAN AS HE SEEKS TREATMENT
(HE'S NEARLY TOTALLY BLIND) FROM THE EXILED DR.
JOSE P. RIZAL.

ONE LOOK AT THE EYES OF TAUFFER,
THE DOCTOR'S OTHER EYE THEN LOOKS AT THE YOUNG
GIRL,
BLUE-EYED FOREIGNER WITH CHESTNUT HAIR!

IS THIS LOVE AT FIRST SIGHT, DOCTOR?
IS SHE THE ONE? WHAT A BEGUILING, EURO-ASIAN BEAUTY!
IS SHE GOING TO BE YOUR EVERLASTING LOVE?

BUT JOSEPHINE B., DADDY NEEDS YOU.
THERE IS NO CURE FOR HIS EYES. YOU HAVE TO TRAVEL
WITH HIM BACK TO HONG KONG AND TO YOUR HOME.

BUT IT WAS ONLY TO MANILA THAT SHE WENT WITH
TAUFER.
JOSEPHINE WENT BACK TO DAPITAN, TO RIZAL'S WAITING
ARMS
BECAUSE SHE HAD ALSO FALLEN IN LOVE..............

LEONOR RIVERA, GUNDING KATIGBAK, ORANG
VALENZUELA,
FILIPINA; CONNIE ORTIGA, SPANISH; O-SEI-KIYO-SAN,
JAPANESE;
AND TOTTIE BECKETT, NELLIE BOUSTEAD, SUZANNE
JACOBY,
ALL FROM EUROPE. MISS B. ASKS, WHY ME?
IS JOE ALREADY SO SAD AND FORLORN HERE? HE'S A
TRAVELLER!

JOSEPHINE B. RIZAL AND JOSEPHINE BRACKEN IN TALISAY!

KISSING HER BESIDE THAT BIG ROCK NEAR THE
SEASHORE…...
LET'S MARRY NOW HERE, BEFORE THE SKIES, BEFORE THE
SEAS,
BEFORE THE WINDS, BEFORE THIS EARTH
AND BEFORE GOD, MY RESTLESS GOLONDRINA,
FOR AUTHORITIES ARE TELLING ME: NO, NO, NO,
DOCTOR RIZAL, NO,
YOU HAVE TO RETRACT FIRST ALL THAT YOU HAVE
WRITTEN
AND SPREAD AGAINST US, BEFORE THE CHURCH
ALLOWS YOUR MARRIAGE TO MISS B.

BUT NO! NEVER, NEVER, NEVER
WILL I DEMEAN MY HONOR, MY FREEDOM, MY WORK, MY
RAGE!
LOVE, I'M SO ALONE HERE, AND OH HOW MY COUNTRY
SUFFERS
BUT TOMORROW….SOMEDAY….SOON…OUR NATION WILL
BE FREE!

JOSEPHINE B. RIZAL AND JOSEPHINE BRACKEN ALL THE WAY!
AT THE HOUSE, IN THE BOYS SCHOOL, AT THE CLINIC AND HOSPITAL,
AT THE FARM, IN BUSINESS, WE HELPED EACH OTHER.
OUR FUTURE IS HERE, THIS IS OUR HOME SWEET HOME!
"NEVER TO PART, HEART BOUND TO HEART!"
AND WHEN OUR BABY FRANCISCO DIED,
GOD, WHY MUST IT BE OUR LITTLE RIZAL?

IT'S NEAR, FORT SANTIAGO IS NEAR,
THE FIRING SQUAD IS NEAR!
"DEAR AND UNHAPPY WIFE"
WE HAD SUCH AN AMAZING YEAR!
"GOOD-BYE, MY SWEET FOREIGNER, MY FRIEND, MY HAPPINESS!"

IT'S TIME TO GO, JOSEPHINE B.
"YOUR EVER FAITHFUL AND TRUE TILL DEATH."
JOSEPHINE B., FAREWELL......
I'VE GOT TO GO......'BYE JO!

JAMMER K.

NOVEMBER 10, 1991
MANILA, PHILIPPINES

SAYANG

Sayang yung katorse anyos
    Na namatay sa droga.

Sayang yung ni-rape na musmos.
    Ayun, tinapon na lang sa ilang
    Na damuhan,
Pinaglaruan muna ng saksak ang murang katawan.

Sayang ang sanggol na nakitang kahalo
    Ng sirang gulay at basura. Throw-away baby 'yan,
Inabort ng ina. Baka dagain o pusain ito sa dram.

Sayang ang nalunod sa Ormoc
    Dahil sa flashflood.
Sayang ang mga patay na isda
    Sa tabing pampang,
    Nabusog yata sa umispil na langis.

Sayang yung patay na ibon.
    Pinatay na bukid, na punong kahoy,
    Palaganap na toxic waste, dahil sa winarak
At inabusong kapaligiran, pinatay na panaginip.
    Mga luray-luray na pag-asa.

Sayang, wala pang sinasampol
    Sa lethal injection.
Sayang, inilibing na yung kinidnap.

Sayang, si Anwar Ibrahim ng Malaysia pa
    Sa isang International Discourse
    Ang nagpadama sa matinding kabayanihan
Ng isang Dr. Jose P. Rizal natin,
    Bayaning pang Asia-Pacific at pang buong mundo yata yan, Sis!

Sayang, wala pang Olympic Games dito sa Pilipinas
    Kasi hindi na binuhay ang bid natin nuon.
Wala pang orig na motor pang sasakyan,
    Gawang Pilipinas. Wala pang petro-chemical plant,
Wala pang nuclear power plant. "Di bale, Choy,
    May orig na OCWs naman, orig na galunggong,
    Orig na batong pang-hilod, orig na streetchildren,
At isama mo na, orig na iskwaters.

Sayang, bago mag-last full show sa sinehan
    Pinaaawit pa ang National Anthem - Lupang Hinirang.
    Hoy, angkop pang nasyonalismo'to!
    "Tumayo tayo, ilagay ang kanang kamay
    Sa dibdib, sa harap ng puso at umawit......"

Sayang napakadaling banggitin:
    "Disiplina", "kultura", "global", "demokrasya",
    "Sustainable Development", "Human Rights",
    "Sovereignty resides in the people".
    Teka, teka muna. Nagtatapon ka ba ng basura
    Ng maayos? Palagian ba ang pagsunod mo sa trapiko?
    Pumipila ka ba gaya ng pag-pila mo sa McDO?
    Pards, konting sakripisyo lang!
Sayang wala pang jury trial dito sa Pilipinas, at least, sa heinous crimes.

Sayang, hanggang ngayon'y di pa naililipat
   Ang mga buto ni Josephine Bracken sa Pilipinas.
   Wala na yatang super lubos na nagmahal kay Rizal
   Na katulad mo. Ngunit, balang araw ....Sweet Foreigner.....
   Balang araw...............malapit na........
   Mapapadito ka na rin sa piling ng..........Dear Joe, Darling Love mo!

                                                    --Ulilangkoboy

Manila, 1998

SAYANG

(A FREE AND UNSTRUCTURED RENDERING IN ENGLISH)

(There is no exact word in the English language for the Philippine
Tagalog word SAYANG.
However, we can be content and admit a free translation of it, such as
"IT'S A PITY", "WHAT A PITY", "WHAT A WASTE" or the
now-a-days groovier, hip "EEEWWW!")

....

IT'S A PITY THAT THE FOURTEEN-YEAR OLD
    DIED OF DRUGS.

IT'S A PITY FOR THE TOT WHO WAS RAPED,
HER FRAGILE BODY, PLAYED WITH A MEDLEY OF KNIFE
WOUNDS,
THROWN AND HIDDEN IN THE GRASSES.
IT'S A THROW-AWAY BABY, ABORTED BY MOTHER!

WHAT A WASTE FOR THE BABY FOUND WITH ROTTEN
VEGETABLES
AND GARBAGE, HEY, CAREFUL, THE RATS OR CATS
MAY COME AND GET IT FROM THE GARBAGE DRUM.

A PITY FOR THOSE WHO DROWNED IN ORMOC, AFTER A
FLASHFLOOD.
PITY THE DEAD FISHES ON RIVER BANKS,
BLOATED AFTER AN OIL SPILL; DEAD BIRDS. PARCHED
FIELDS
AND FARMS, WILTED TREES; AND THE INCREASE IN
TOXIC WASTE
BECAUSE OF THE ABUSE AND DEGRADATION OF THE
ENVIRONMENT,

KILLING DREAMS AND LEAVING BUT TATTERED HOPES.
PITY THERE IS STILL NO SAMPLING OF EXECUTION BY
LETHAL INJECTION.
PITY, THEY'RE BURYING THE KIDNAP VICTIM NOW.

PITY IT WAS ANWAR IBRAHIM OF MALAYSIA
WHO EXTOLLED, IN AN INTERNATIONAL DISCOURSE,
THE MARTYRDOM OF OUR NATIONAL HERO, DR. JOSE. P.
RIZAL,
WHO BELONGS TO ASIA-PACIFIC AND TO THE WORLD!

PITY THERE IS YET NO OLYMPIC GAMES HELD IN THE
PHILIPPINES.
NOBODY EVER FOLLOWED UP OUR BID TO HOST ONE.
WE HAVE NO ORIGINAL CAR MOTOR, MADE IN THE
PHILIPPINES;
NO PETRO-CHEMICAL PLANT, NO NUCLEAR POWER
PLANT.
BUT NO MATTER, WE HAVE ORIGINAL OCWS;
ORIGINAL BODY STONE SCRUB, ORIGINAL GALUNGGONG-
FISH,
ORIGINAL STREETCHILDREN, AND INCLUDE ALSO--
ORIGINAL SQUATTERS!

WHAT A PITY, BEFORE THE LAST FULL SHOW IN MOVIE
HOUSES,
WE ARE CALLED TO SING OUR LUPANG HINIRANG--
NATIONAL ANTHEM.
HEY BRO., THIS ONE'S FOR THE NATIONALISM! "ALL
STAND UP,
PLACE YOUR RIGHT HAND IN FRONT OF YOUR HEART
AND SING…"

EEEWWW! HOW WE CAN EASILY SAY---
"DISCIPLINE", "CULTURE", "HERITAGE", "GLOBAL",
"DEMOCRACY", "COMPETITIVENESS", "SUSTAINABLE
DEVELOPMENT",
"HUMAN RIGHTS", AND "SOVEREIGNTY RESIDES IN THE
PEOPLE"---
BUT WAIT PLEASE, ARE YOU THROWING GARBAGE
PROPERLY? DO YOU ALWAYS FOLLOW TRAFFIC RULES OR
FALL IN LINE
LIKE YOU'D DO AT MCDO? MAKE SOME LITTLE SACRIFICE,
FRIEND.
PITY, THERE IS YET NO JURY TRIAL IN THE PHILIPPINES,
EVEN FOR HEINOUS CRIMES.

A PITIFUL EPISODE--UNTIL NOW THE BONES OF
JOSEPHINE BRACKEN
HAVE NOT BEEN TRANSFERRED AND BURIED IN THE
PHILIPPINES.
THERE NEVER WAS A WOMAN LIKE HER
WHO SO UNABASHEDLY BESTOWED HER ETERNAL LOVE
FOR RIZAL!
IN THE FUTURE...SWEET FOREIGNER...IN SOME FUTURE
TIME...
AND PRETTY SOON...YOU WILL BE HERE...WITH YOUR
DEAR JOE...
YOUR DARLING LOVE!

                                        --ULILANGKOBOY

July 2, 2006
Orlando, Fl

PUSHCART BABY: A TALE IN MANILA

There was a baby born inside a pushcart in Manila.
  The father, a shoe repairman, assisted his wife deliver the baby.
Now the family: husband, wife, a daughter,
  And the baby, live, eat, and sleep
Inside the wooden vehicle. When the rains fall, and pour hard,
  The four people cramp themselves inside.

Juan Cruz Nabong Jr.

TIMELESS VOICES
The International Library of Poetry
poetry.com, One Poetry Plaza
Owings Mills, MD 21117
2006

The above photo was taken during our OPLAN ERMITA ON STREETCHILDREN. Picture shows streetchildren with some of my team members; woman social workers led by Miss Mauricia Dancel. My wife Zeny beside me on my right; Rick Isidro the fearless news reporter; and beside him Caesar Agustin, the proponent of the Caesar's Theory". We do work sometimes at night. There were then around 5,000 malnourished and underweight (many abandoned/forgotten by parents) pitifully surviving streetchildren in Manila, mostly in the Ermita and slum areas. These children beg, steal, rob, snatch handbags, pickpockets, beat other children, do drugs, do prostitution, become victims of pedophiles, sexually abused/molested and are seriously affected when they live in areas where there are armed conflicts or insurgency. This operation is one of the "MANILA ON THE GO!" Projects of MAYOR MEL LOPEZ of Manila. The author once chaired the Board of the Father O'Brien Angels Home Foundation.

Love others as God
Loves you
God bless you
Mc Teresa mc

On February 8, 1978, 8:00 o'clock in the evening, at the Missionaries of Charity in Tayuman, Tondo, Manila, upon my request, Mother Teresa sat down beside me after shaking my hand, and gave me her autograph.

THE SIGMA RHO HYMN

FOR THE SIGMA RHO ALL OUR LIFE AND LOYALTY,
LET THY TRADITIONS BE, LIVE FIRMER AS THE FREE;
GIRD LIFE WITH THE TRUTH, BROTHERS LOVE WITHIN
THY ROOTS,
IN SERVICE GLAD AS SPRING, WHAT ZEALOUS SPIRIT CLINGS.

WE'LL REMEMBER THEE AFTER WE HAVE GONE
TO FACE LIFE'S BURDENS AND JOYS;
ETERNAL ONENESS IN DEEPEST NEEDS,
DREAMS, DEEDS OF YOUTH SO BOLD!

FOR THE SIGMA RHO, TIMELESS SEEKERS OF THE RIGHT,
IMBUE PEACE AS WE STRIVE, REAP HONOR WITH GOOD
FIGHT,
TO OUR BROTHERHOOD, MEN OF TRUST AND WILL AND
BLOOD;
SO FERVENT WITH BRIGHT HOPES, OUR FAITH IN THEE
UPHOLD!

TO THE END!!!
FOR THE SIGMA RHO!!! FIGHT!!! FOR THE GRAND
ARCHON!!! FIGHT!!!

MUSIC: BROD JOE ABEJO
LYRICS: BROD JOHNNY NABONG
ARRANGED BY: PROF. LUCIO SAN PEDRO
IN 1980

U.P. DILIMAN, QUEZON CITY
PHILIPPINES 1955

THE IBP HYMN

WE MOVE WITH A DREAM, DEDICATED TO THE RULE OF
LAW;
FOR TRUTH IS SUPREME, TO THE GOOD THE LIGHT
BESTOW.

WE'LL LEAD WITH A FAITH, OUR PROFESSIONS'S
STANDARDS ELEVATE;
JUSTICE WILL LIVE, OUR PUBLIC DUTY GIVE.

LET US DEVELOP AN EFFECTIVE BENCH AND BAR,
WELCOME ALL LAWYERS FOR LEADERSHIP;
COME WITH INTEGRITY, FAIRNESS, AND COMPETENCE,
BE TRUE TO YOUR LEARNING AND SOCIAL CONSCIENCE.

WE CARE WITH A LOVE, ALL OUR HEARTS TO JUSTICE
BEAT;
BE STRONG IT WILL EVER BE,
THE INTEGRATED BAR, THE INTEGRATED BAR
OF THE PHILIPPINES!!!

MUSIC: ATTY. JOSE B. ABEJO
LYRICS: ATTY. JUAN C. NABONG JR.

MANILA, PHILIPPINES
1982

UPLAA DIAMOND JUBILEE SONG

THE DREAMS, YES, THE CHALLENGES OUR FOUNDERS SAW,
GREAT MOMENTS TO BUILD A GLORIOUS COLLEGE OF LAW;
AND ON THIS DAY WE PAUSE, WE PRAISE OUR MENTORS'
DEEDS,
REMEMBERING, CHERISHING THE WORK OF THE U.P.
COLLEGE OF LAW.

RELENTLESS LOVE OF LAW AND HONOR ENNOBLES THE
MIND,
ZEALOUS, FEARLESS DEVOTION TO DUTY IN OUR HEARTS
ENSHRINED;
TRADITION, FREEDOM AND FAIRNESS BLAZINGLY SHINE,
WHEN CHARTING LIGHT IN THE TRESTLEBOARD OF LIFE.

BEHOLD THOSE DREAMS! U.P. LAW ALUMNI ASSOCIATION,
NOW!
LOVE AND SERVICE TO RIGHTNESS THY VISION BE;
WE MUST RENEW THE FAITH, FAILED VIRTUES SAVE,
GUIDE US EVER TO FOREVER UPHOLD TRUTH'S TENETS
SUPREME!

MUSIC: DEAN RAMON SANTOS
U.P. COLLEGE OF MUSIC

LYRICS: JUAN C. NABONG JR.
U.P. LAW '58

DILIMAN, 1985

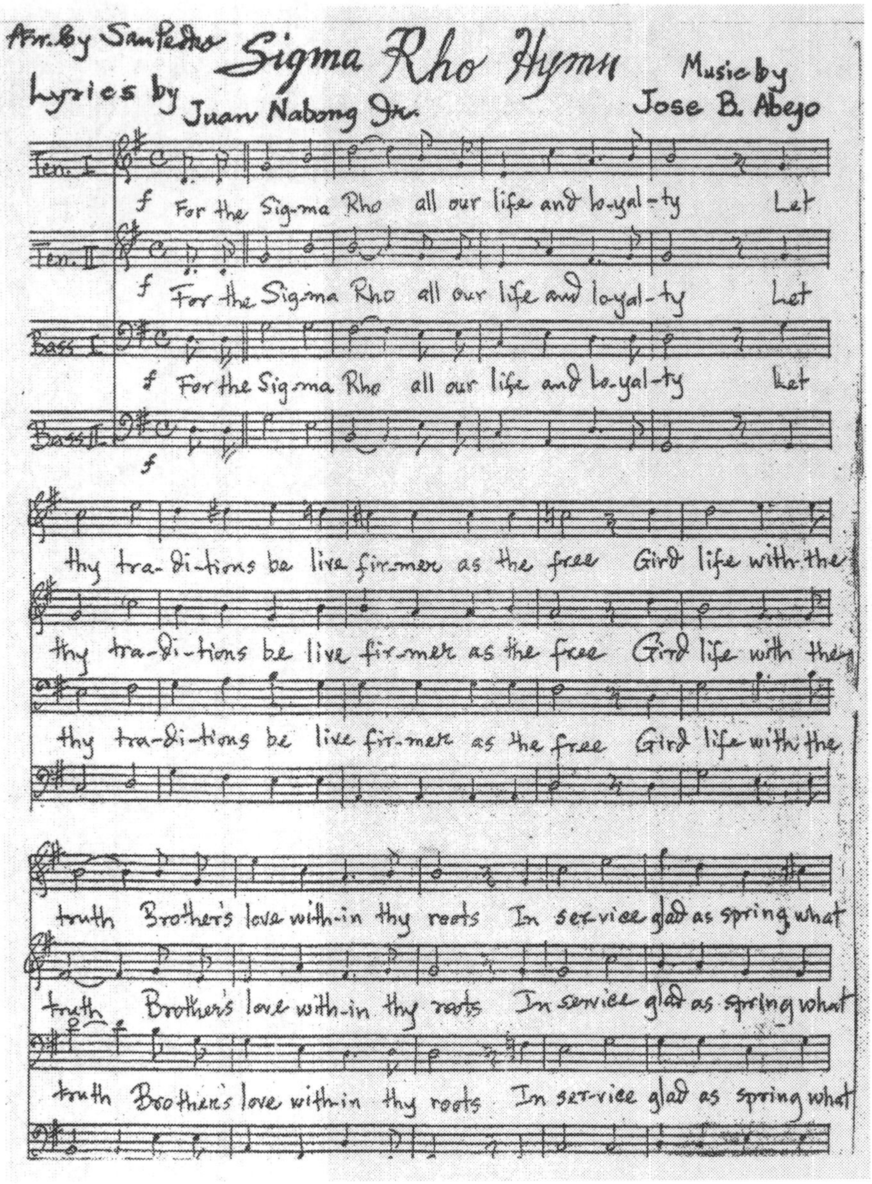

zealous spirit clings.

zealous spirit clings.

zealous spirit clings. We'll re-member thee after we have gone To

face life's burdens and joys   E-ternal one-ness in

free life's burdens and joys   E-ternal one-ness in

face life's burdens and joys   E-ternal one-ness in

deepest needs. Dreams, deeds of youth so bold.   For the Sig-ma

deepest needs. Dreams, deeds of youth so bold.   For the Sig-ma

deepest needs   Dreams, deeds of youth so bold.   For the Sig-ma

Rho— Timeless seekers of the Right Im-bue peace as we strive Reap

honor with good fight   To our Brother-hood Men of

trust and will and blood   So fer-vent with bright hopes our

46

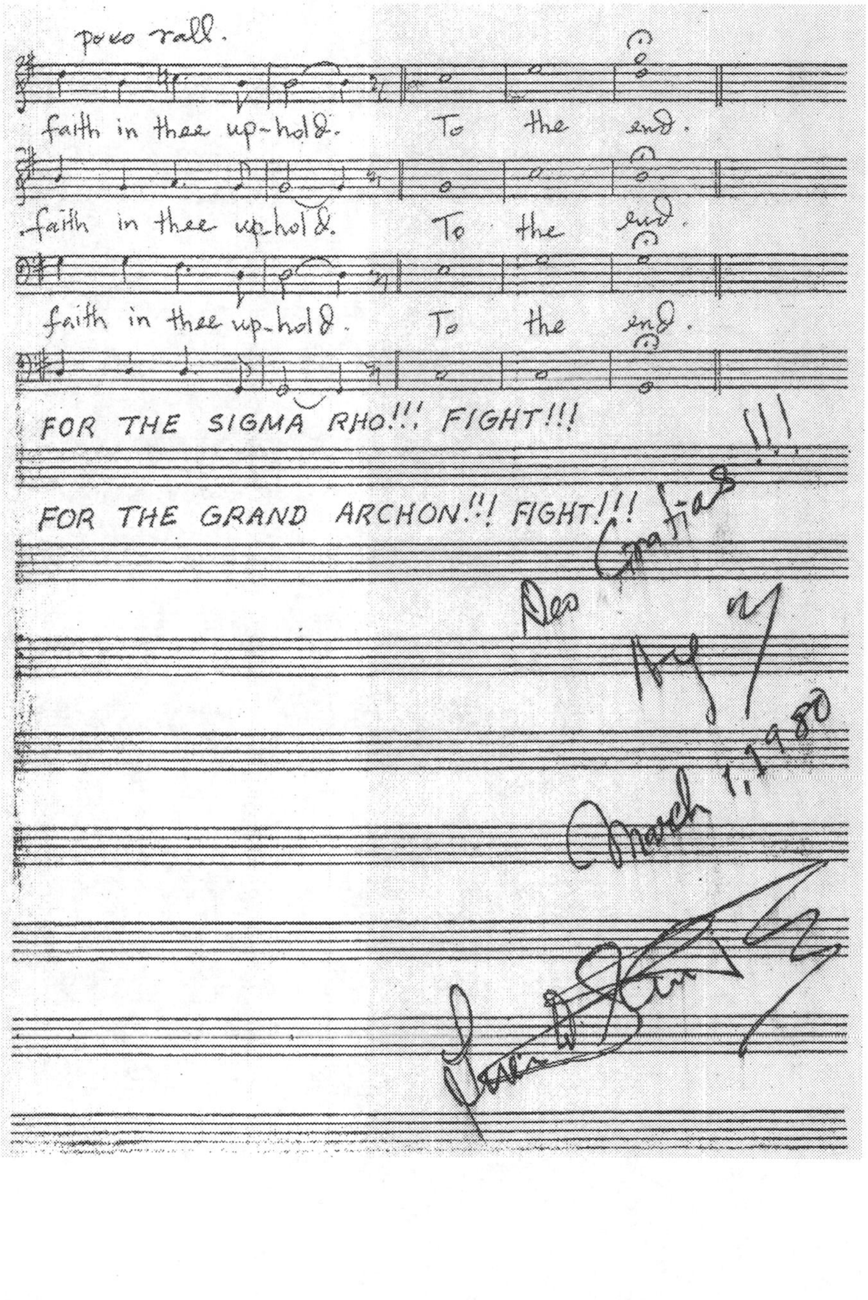

poco rall.
faith in thee up-hold. To the end.
faith in thee up-hold. To the end.
faith in thee up-hold. To the end.
faith in thee up-hold. To the end.
FOR THE SIGMA RHO!!! FIGHT!!!
FOR THE GRAND ARCHON!!! FIGHT!!!
Deo Gratias!!!
March 1, 1980

"The IBP Hymn"

Words by: ATTY. Juan C. Nabong Jr.   Music by: ATTY. Jose B. Abejo

We move with a dream, De-di-ca-ted to the Rule of Law; for Truth is su-preme, To the Good the Light bes-tow. We'll lead with a faith, our pro-fes-sion's standards e-le-vate; jus-tice will live, our pub-lic Du-ty give. Let us de-ve-lop an ef-fec-tive Bench and Bar, Wel-come all

The IBP Hymn

law - yers for lead - er - ship ; come with in - te - gri - ty,

fair-ness, and com - pe - tence, Be true to your learn - ing and

so - cial cons - cience; We care with a Love, All our

hearts to jus - tice beat ; Be strong it will e - ver be, the In - te -

grated Bar, the In - te - gra - ted Bar of the Phi - lip -

pines!

48   4/9/81

49